1+1=5

and Other Unlikely Additions

by David LaRochelle

illustrated by Brenda Sexton

STERLING

New York / London

To the Delton Group and the KTM crew:
faithful friends and wonderful writers. —D. L.

To Mr. P, the smile in my life. —B. S.

Library of Congress Cataloging-in-Publication Data
LaRochelle, David.
 1+1=5 : and other unlikely additions / by David LaRochelle ; illustrated by Brenda Sexton.
    p. cm.
 ISBN 978-1-4027-5995-6
 1. Addition--Juvenile literature. I. Sexton, Brenda, ill. II. Title. III. Title: One plus one equals five.
 QA115.L37 2010
 513.2'11--dc22

                                          2009040873

Lot#: 10 9 8 7 6 5 4 3 2 1
03/10

Published by Sterling Publishing Co., Inc.
387 Park Avenue South, New York, NY 10016
Text copyright © 2010 by David LaRochelle
Illustration copyright © 2010 Brenda Sexton
Distributed in Canada by Sterling Publishing
c/o Canadian Manda Group, 165 Dufferin Street
Toronto, Ontario, Canada M6K 3H6
Distributed in the United Kingdom by GMC Distribution Services
Castle Place, 166 High Street, Lewes, East Sussex, England BN7 1XU
Distributed in Australia by Capricorn Link (Australia) Pty. Ltd.
P.O. Box 704, Windsor, NSW 2756, Australia

Printed in China

Sterling ISBN 978-1-4027-5995-6

For information about custom editions, special sales, premium and
corporate purchases, please contact Sterling Special Sales
Department at 800-805-5489 or specialsales@sterlingpublishing.com.

Designed by Brenda Sexton and Chrissy Kwasnik
The artwork was prepared digitally

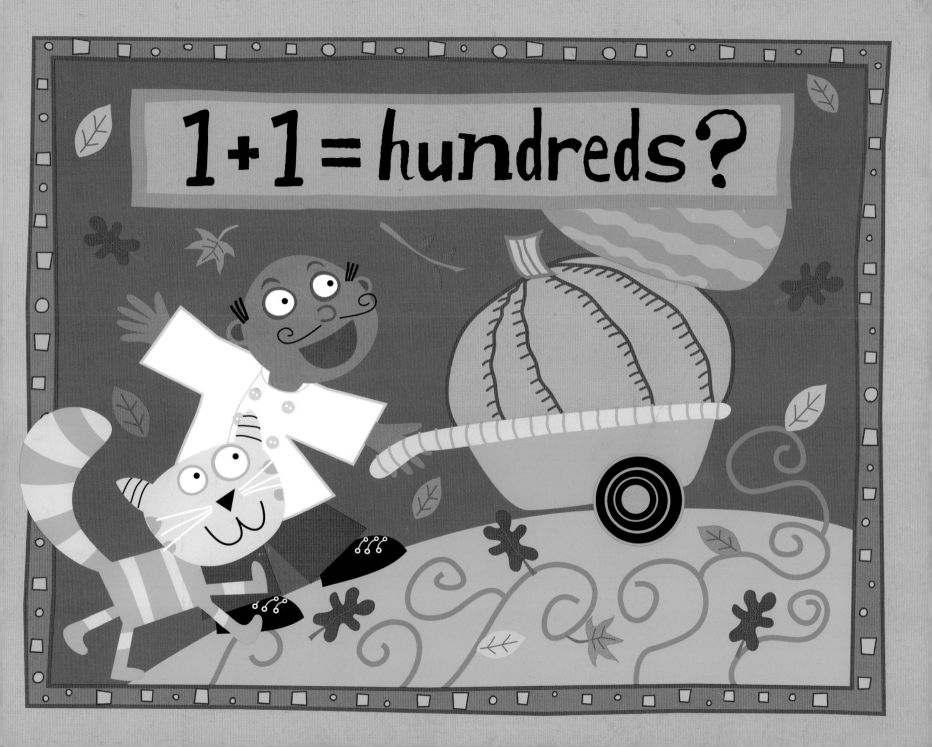

1 a.m. + 1 p.m. = 1 day!

1wheelchair + 1skateboard = 8wheels!

1 left foot + 1 right foot = 10 toes!